AF199747

COFFEE SHOP DIARIES

I

j. t. baka

Ukiyo-e

prologue

me

born early

to live a long fullfilling life

at midnight

doors and gates

opening to the singing

of a mute nightingale

born late

to live a short life

ending with a wham bang

at midnight

a pregnant ghost

dancing to the sound

of a violin playing goat

stillborn

to live a life among the stars

at midnight

a lady fox and a deer

starting to travel the milky way

to the sound of their heartbeats

born right at midnight

a wanderer between worlds

living many lives

who are

you

out in the cold

white night

and where

under

the bright shining stars

non-place.*requiem*

catching up

in between

dead ends

dead ends

in between

in between

dead ends

dead ends

in between

in between

dead ends

dead ends

in between

in

between dead

ends

dead ends

dead

end

desire

struggling

strangled

what's the difference

hired

fired

what's the difference

eat

eaten

what's the difference

kill

killed

what's the difference

building

destroying

what's the difference

start a relationship

finish a relationship

what's the difference

loved

hated

what's the difference

if there is no one

make one

together

brace yourself

for the grace

of a place

full of love for itself

and you

yes and you

brace yourself

for the face

you are going to encounter

at the counter

brace yourself

for the haze

you are going to fall into

before falling in love

with the grace of a face

you are going to faze

because

all of a sudden

it's a chase through a maze

and the clock is ticking

and evil is licking

it's lips

ready for the dips

you are going to deliver

start not to shiver

and do not quiver

don't be fazed

by the face

welcome her grace

and you will come out of the maze

with her

together

yes together

BRACE

IMPACT IMMANENT

I am

gonna treat

you

I am

gonna feed

(me)

you

my heart

singing

in the shower

with all of my heart

smiled upon

by the morning sun

touched

by her golden rays

which are forming

a pair of a horse and a deer

dancing on my skin

embraced

by her warmth

I am readying

myself for the beauty

of the day

with all of my being

standing

in front of the counter

smiled upon

by the barista

touched

by the warmth of her smile

embraced

by the happiness in her eyes

I delight

in a vision of

us together

now and forever for just a second

sitting at the table

at the window

staring into the cup

of hot steaming coffee

watching the steam

forming into a pair

of a horse and a deer

dancing around each other

anticipating the coffee's strong taste

with delight

while enjoying the sweet taste of a danish
pastry

I am readying

myself for today's challenges

but

by a stroke of bad luck

by a stroke of the poet's brush

I am suddenly

spiraling down into madness

ending

in a pit full of sadness

the deadness

of reality

I was

there before

I was

there before already

here

in this very spot

and that

more than once

to tell you the truth

you fool

encore

love's

a whore

love's

a bore

requires

no

encore

but

asks

for more

until

there is

no more

cause

all

there is

is gore

ENCORE

enslaved

on the wall

a mirror

bleeding

tears

outlining

a face

on the wall

a face

mirroring

a blackened heart

burnt

into the ground

a shadow's shadow

of a love

blinded

by a future

shown in the mirror

on the wall

no go areas

kyeongbukgung

deoksugung

the baker's table

a twosome place

paris baguette

what's

left

what the book?

coffee to go

a twosome place – revisited

standing in front

of an empty space of place

that actually isn't empty

but what was there

is gone

literally gone

leaving behind just memories of it

and emptiness

emptiness

where my heart

used to be

realization setting in

there are places

that I can't go to

because I lost the right to do so

there are places

that I can't go to

because the love

that used to be there

moved on

but there are also places

I can't go to anymore

but need them still to be there

to exist

and that are

gone

literally GONE

not a long time ago

there was someone saying

there is a difference between

a person gone

and a person gone

back then

I didn't agree

but standing in front of the empty space

full of emptiness myself

I realize there may be truth to it

on the other hand

it doesn't change the fact

of being left

out

of being

left

behind

the hug cafe

more

than a year later

walking

by the window

more

by accident

than anything else

taking

a look inside

more

by accident

than anything else

the owner working

a baby strapped to her chest closely

mother and child

smiling

laughing happily

journey

railroad tracks

running

all the way

up north

losing themselves

in the cold of a winter's morning

they were covered in ice

running

all the way

up north

they were losing themselves

in the nebula of a winter's morning

until

a bright cold sun

cleared the sky

but all too soon

the cold bright day

gave way

to a mist

travelling along

the railroad track's path

at breakneck speed

encroaching the sun

soon

the temperature dropped

and a death-cold darkness

engulfed the sun

soon

snow started to fall

covering

the railroad tracks

the railroad tracks

running all the way

up north

losing themselves in the growing stream of
black pain

a scream

followed by a spray of red gold

splashing on the railroad tracks

intermingling with the snow flakes

still falling

on the railroad tracks

the railroad tracks

running

all the way

up north

in complete darkness

to an unknown destination

in the aurora borealis of hurt

16. **A**

a quick one

hollowed

who

am I

and

if yes

where

am I

shallowed

by kind permission of

down under

down by the water

I lie there buried in summerday sands

helpless

like a beached whale

wrecked on the shore

down under

down by the water

I am trying to find my way

through a maze of voices and lights I am

trapped in

down under

down by the water

I see occasional happiness popping up the
waves

riding them clueless like driftwood

like me

down under

down by the water

I am looking into the sun

drowning in its ocean of livid heat

trying to escape

down under

down by the water

watching the sky

I feel a wind coming up

with it

the wind brings the smell of distant rain

and the promise of something new

a change of season

a change of clothes

a change of live

down under

down by the water

on the beach

or anywhere else

mayhem maybe

living

sitting on the train

on my way to watch

bunnys playing football

I see a woman walking by the window

walking down the platform

on her way to the exit

I can see her only from behind

to tell the truth

all I see

all

I can see

is her beautiful ass

I can't stop staring

at her beautiful shaped bottocks

usually the wrong pair

of trousers or jeans

are trying everything to make you look

bad from behind

but in the case of the woman

vanishing up the stairs of the exit

the pair of jeans is doing everything

to show off the beauty of her bottom

I didn't see her face

I didn't know her name

I didn't ask for her number

I just enjoyed the view

simple

as that

nothing

more

but

nothing less as well

life

can be beautiful

labyrinth

what if

the abyss

is just a wall in front of you

what if

the wall

is the beginning of a way

what if

the wall

is the road to your final destinition

and not just the first step into a maze

but what if

the final destination

turns out to be just a stop-over

and what if

the stop-over

is another wall

and what if

there are walls all around you

and what if

the cell you find yourself in

is a black hole of emptiness

but

what if

the emptiness

is just a feeling

just a feeling

a feeling like

love

leftover

cruising through

a dream

like cutting through

a scream

love my dark angel

on each corner

on each traffic light

I see the same woman

with her smile so bright

love my dark angel

floating through

clouds

like living as a shroud

next to my plane

I see game

an angel following me

baring her fangs

she is smiling

beguiling

love my dark angel

driving through

waves of illusions

like scathing through

hope just hatched

enlightening darkness

encouraging blackwholeness

love my dark angel

where did she go

where

did I

get lost

love my dark angel

all that's left

a carcass of my love

surrounded by dark angels

feasting on the rotten flash

eating their own

love

my

dark

watching you

watching me

watching an animation on my mobile

the joker

on the move

on a rampage

coming closer and closer

watching me

getting uncomfortable

watching me

trying to stop the animation

the joker gets it

the joker talks to me

if I really wanna stop

and why

he is asking me

watching me

getting animated

more and more

watching me

pressing the off button

nothing is happening

but the joker pressing his case

he is coming

closer and closer

watching me

getting agitated

more and more

I am pressing the off button

knowing my mother is near

feeling it

I know

my mother is close

feeling

nothing really bad

can happen

I still push the button

until the mobile breaks

watching

pieces falling

watching

tears falling

awakening

slowly realizing

it was just a dream

slowly realizing

I am here still

while my mother is long gone

remembering

tears are still streaming down my cheeks

remembering

tears are still falling down to earth

watching them

still falling on my mother's grave

watching me

still crying

déjà vu in memoriam

at a lake house

a hitch in time

and a crack opened up the dawn

velvet darkness bleeding through

at a lake house

a glitch in space

and a crack in the dawn opened up

blackened blood pouring through

at a lake house

a stitch in life

and a cracked dawn opened up

sacred darkness seeping through

at a lake house

a snitch in love

slicing down the dawn in two

sacrificed blood splashing through

standing under

a cracking dome of gold

I watch tears running along it cracks

coming together in the void of my heart

until it bursts

screaming

I stand crying

in the eye of the storm

watching the shift

in the gravity

of my soul

she was

all that

and now

I am a wrecked stranger

in the ruin of a foreign life

 a desert

in a winter snowscape

burning

under the holy glow of ice and snow

into a undead carcass of eternal suffering

of love

lessness

excess

tessness

in a heartbeat of a deadbeat

I scream me to sleep

to cry you a song

imagine

all the dead people

happy birthday

mr wyler

the truth

tomorrow

is a bridge

too far

eternity

on the other hand

is just

a small step away

just an inch

actually

just

a moment

just

a breath

16. **B**

kappa

wonderful arms with hands

long beautiful fingers

strong long legs with feet

of round-shaped tiny toes

a body

sleek and slick

stream-lined to conquer

the blues of heaven and sea

with wings of a bat

losing myself in the way

of the window sill

walking along its edge

skating along the water's edge

dancing alone above its shore

until falling

head oder heels

keeling over and over

and over myself

through the air

until splashing and crashing

in the Cambrian Sea

with a glee

waking me

up

and finding myself

under a penguin's foot

swimming in my own blood

smashed

going the way of a jabberwock

although

all that really

happened was

run over by a future's past

like a stray

that I was

going back

one of the baristas

is cleaning the table

next to ours

she is wearing

a badge

showing everyone

what's not showing yet

it's not the first time

at a starbucks

you see a barista

wearing that badge

and pregnant baristas

at starbucks

are nothing to you

it was the one at

a twosome place

wearing no badge whatsoever

who is still

haunting you

I see

even on a sunny day

darkness prevails

even on a happy day

clouds snuffing out the sunlight

even on a dark day

there was no end to laughter after

even on a day before

the opposite looms bright

but later on

we will all be gone

like the dead

that never lived

big

now let the past

take a hit

and let the days go by

just wave

and say

hi

tomorrow will be

yesterday

the day after tomorrow

so no sorrow

zorro

likewise

just like

the stars

just like

the moon

just like

the sun

just like

the blue in the sky

just like

the cotton candy of clouds

just like

heaven

just like

the snow-capped mountains

just like

the deep blue of a mountain lake

just like

the peace of a mountain forest

just like

the light of a clearing in a mountain forest

just like

the golden green of grass in a clearing

just like

paradise

just like

you

just like

me

just like

us together

just like

a long story just about to begin

like

a flickering candle

snuffed out

just like

death

just

like me

can I go home now

sleeping

dreaming

when I was young

I was in a garden

following its path

the flowers the trees the grass darkened

with every step I took

their colours faded away

green red blue changed into black

and like all things living

the sky turned dark

while I was walking along the garden's path

the sun vanished

behind dark clouds

the golden sunrays cut off for good

while I was walking along the garden's path

it started to snow

the leaves crumbled in the cold

the plants withered away

and the garden turned into an ashen desert

and with every step

taken

the ashen landscape turned into
nothingness

under my heavy boots

not even dust remained

dreaming

screaming

sitting on a fence one day

overlooking a garden

in winter

while looking into the white darkness

a light is piercing through the black clouds

and the sun is sending golden rays of light
down

everything

it touches turns

into colour

into light

the grass the trees the flowers

blossom

and all of a sudden I stare at something

that feels like hope

I discover details

I never saw

when I was young

I never saw the potential

that was right there

in front of me

in the garden of my soul

now I understand

why it might be better

if the translator of a text

is older

than its writer

42

behind me

a flight with a stop in between

a long flight

crossing continents but not oceans

and now

in front of me

two pieces of cake

for one

bridging the gap

in between

waiting for the pick-up

listening to a couple

next table

with their mothers talking

about weight limits

once there was a time

when I was sitting here

with my mother

but that was

then

now

I am just here

to pay

my taxes

for now I am in between

and listening to the female half of the
couple

talking about her father

time changes

everything

even the coffee shop

I went to with my mother then

has a different name now

how familiar

only guys in between

stay the same

posthumously

when number

9 was

the last in line

it was the last day

of 5

in a row of teaching

but it

was also

the last day of 2

on the other hand

the first one to go

was the last one to stand

in number 9

how ironic

and iconic

when you think of it

all you need is greed

and CGI

vorbei vorbei

at last

out of touch

the closer I get

to reaching my goal

the more it gets

out of reach

talking about

perfection

shall we

mixed zone

a variation on jeffrey's

after the hare

found his spectacles

he became aware

that his was

the story of the writer

who didn't

read his own works

it was not

because he had lost his spectacles

it was

that he had lost his spectacles

because of that

maybe

because

who knows

the hare

was such

a scatterbrained wuss

sometimes

structured 1

maybe

in all those

years

a hope will never

zero

all that is full of

kindness

indeed

a hope indeed will rise

o hell yes or o hell no

in whom you trust

wether

all is lost

shall not distract you now

hope is

everything

regardless

everything else

gitane

jet lagged

I am dreaming

of a tank

driving along

an empty road

in the center of the city

in the middle of the night

coming straight at me

the tank stopps

after I stopped my car

and got out

I am going straight

for the tank driver

sitting on the turret of his tank

smoking a cigarette

relaxing and idle

while shouting in his direction

I am realizing

the tank is actually

an elephant

the elephant in the room

clad in armour

not invisible but invincible

the loneliness of a man

smoking a cigarette

alone in his office

structured 2

inside the heart of the desert is still hope

journey along the desire of your longing

until you meet her

next to a well

go

in peace

with her help

all that is will

surface

here in this very spot

endless calm will be your

reward

endless suffering will end

together you will drink

of the well's water

ookini

the rabbit and the fox

just before nightfall

a snowstorm covered

the mountain range

and everything there

under a thick white fluffy blanket

after the storm lost all his power

in this part of the realm

he went off to another

to rage on again

it was then

that the moon left her house

turning the snowscape with her light

into a world of fairies

snow spirits were dancing

with ghosts of ice

pregnant with hope

for a new age of their kind

ice ghouls were courting

spectres of snow

full of the fiercest cold

it was then

that the rabbit left the safety of his hole

driven by an urge of a need

he did not know

only when

the rabbit in his hunt

for the unknown

looked up

he realized

what he was looking for

the moon

he was staring at

mesmerized

until

he woke up

finding himself

embraced by a sleeping snow fox

panic-stricken

he tried to free himself

only to wake up the fox

who just hugged him more tight

like you couldn't stop

losing yourself in the beauty of the moon

and thereby losing yourself to the cold of
the night

I couldn't stop

losing myself in the beauty of yours

the fox whispered soothingly

caressing the rabbit gently

so you

saved me from the cold

the rabbit asked the fox

still uncertain what to think

yes

I did

she answered his question

by bringing you here

and where

is that

he asked

watching her closely

where does a rabbit live

my love

your dream

of course

which became my dream

naturally

and from which

there is no escape possible

she said

with a smile full of tears

looking from him

into the sun of a new dawn

a knife's vision

in a black room I see

a smaller black room

mirroring darkness

a small girl I see

sitting in front of the smaller room

a small girl

emitting darkness

a small girl

cuddling a black teddy bear

a black teddy bear

with her eyes

staring into the void of the empty space

inside her

the empty space

a black wormhole

where her heart used to be

now a live-sucking emptiness

 sending out

waves of never-ending sadness

sitting on its shore

I watch the waves

hitting the beach

the corona

around the empty space of my heart

a memory

gone mad after going berserk

a heart

lost

in sorrow and pain

of a black room

in a space made out of the darkness

of my raped soul

are you there

still

in the closet

structured 3

all that is

nevertheless

determinates what is to come

indeed

wether you like it or not

and you have to be prepared for that

saturdays and sundays as well

hope will help you

everywhere with what you have to do

right now and

every step along the way

and you will

see

with every step taken

ending it will not make it

less painfull

looking for what you should be

the works

marking

the playing field

describing

the scenery

setting

the mood

picturing

the characters

starting

the action

telling

the story

checking

the plot points

working out

the motifs

playing along

their tune

letting

the choir sing the chorus line

hitting

the marks

repeating

the formula with variations in taste and
colour

repeating

until rebooting

time

and again dear fren

vienna

common sense

it should have been

easy as pie

and

actually it was

although there was

a storm

and many flights got

cancelled

but the bus

came and brought you to the airport

and the plane at the airport

brought you to your destination

from there

cat and the subway

brought you to the gasometer

and it was only then

that you lost direction

that you lost

your way

and ended up

in crozon

and no dolphin

to save you

monsieur aquaman

DB

after coming back

from the concert

of a metal band

that celebrated its 25th anniversary in 2018

according to

the singer

the widow of my father asked me

how it was

what

could I

have said

the first time

I went to

a concert of that very band

was more

than 20 years ago

almost no youth

and no corpse paint at all

but white beards

and pot bellies

(plenty)

that is

how

it is now

and at least

it wasn't going to

a concert of a band

that is much older

like DP

no no no

really shocking

was

something else

although I

have all their albums

I recognized

only one song

they played

it was like my father

said hello

when he came with me

to concerts of JT

he waited just for one

or two songs

of their most famous album

that's

how

it was

for him then

that's

how

it is

for me now

no running with the wolves

anymore

no

wolves in the throne room

anymore

(they are a great band though)

no staying ahead

of the game

anymore

just

a grey wolf lost

on the other hand

maybe

the game

is not important

any longer

but if

so

if that

how

it really is

now

what then

am I doing here

in vienna

waiting for a concert

of young metal foxes

to begin

JT knows

since 1976

walking

through the city

everything

looks so pretty

H & M

Benetton

Starbucks

McDonald's

dm

Thalia

Rituals

Media Markt

OBI

Nordsee

it is all

here

it is all

there

where I just came

from

only the buildings

telling me

this is VIENNA

Stephansdom

Burgtheater

Hofburg

and so on and so forth and so

on and so forth

and Hofer

of course

it's nice

to have a singer

who can still sing

but no surprise

she is not even 30

what was definitely

not nice

that they played

just sixty minutes

staying three days

for sixty minutes

but as it happened

the place

I stay in

became the main event

the place

I stay in

VIENNA

that is

sitting in a coffee shop

thinking about the last month

thinking about the last two days

just one more day

is something to wish for

but truth to be told

it is the short time

making it nice

making it worthwile

and being just on visit

on vacation

that is

remember last time

what

a relieve it was

to leave the plane in incheon

to be back in seoul

to be

back in

korea

but

it would be

nice

nonetheless

just one more day

in vienna

and one more life

too

could have gone

to many museums

there are so many

interesting ones

but the most interesting exhibition

starts only tomorrow

and to tell the truth

it was a bad museum's day today

but still

Schiele was calling

so Leopold it was

after Albertina yesterday

Chagall was calling

then

but after seeing a Schiele

and a Feininger for real

it was time

a book

discovered yesterday

wanted to be bought

at the bookstore

it was a difficult decision

the book was

about Hedy Lemarr

you know

but

carrying it

reading it

when a book about

her was read

in english

already

and already

there was

tomorrow looming

today going back

to germany

tomorrow going back

to korea

the weight limit for that flight

already met

and of cource

the budget

for the trip

to vienna

couldn't forget

that one

so

no book

though there was

more than one

second look though

and the mood

was shoot

and still

so much time left

but the mood

was not good

it was time to leave

and grieve

who know's

it could have been

different

travelling with my loved

one

but there is no

one

no one

travelling with me

no one

waiting for me

not in germany

nor in korea

there is nobody

but me

I guess

waiting at the airport

alone

at the airport

again

from one airport

to the other

so it was

yesterday

but right now

it's the same airport

in less than twelve hours

came yesterday

go today

the same woman

welcoming me

yesterday

today

she said

her good-byes

a year ago

exactly

the beginning of the end

a clock started ticking

but today

before she drove me

to the airport

she asked me

when will you be back

maybe

there is

still some hope

left

from one airport

to another

running

under a cover of grey clouds

full of rain

hiding

behind a window

covered with crystals of ice

bathing in the sun

sparkling

gliding

through white mountains of ice

capped in cold

diving

into a blue unknown

crashing

into a grey mess

losing control

and smashing

head on

in a white dune of feathers

looking around

I find myself

stranded in a desert of clouds

sprinkled

with stardust

happy

to be alive

from one airport

to the other

to another

from vienna

to dusseldorf

just to say good-bye

and move on

come to go

move on

to another airport

just to move on

to another airport

just to come

to say good-bye

and that

on a valentine's day

from one airport

to the other

from one stop-over

to the other

from one

life

to the next

dream

somewhere

from one airport

to the other

oh vienna

four airports

in as many days

oh dusseldorf

four cities

in as many airports

oh helsinki

four countries

as in many cities

oh incheon

from one airport

to the other

running or hiding

hide and seek

or

seek and destroy

cover-up

for

a flop-up

avoiding

hiding

on the run

that's what I become

just a decoy

a decoy for

myself

an illusion

nice hat

nice watch

nice looks

nicer next destination even

believing

just in the deception

for the inception

oh vienna

oh dusseldorf

oh helsinki

oh incheon

from one

hell to another

nowhere to hide

anymore

since I am back

in 김강최국

but wait

an escape hatch

right in front of me

osaka

gateway

to heaven

vision
of a different life

encouragement
for the next round

'cause
it's not over yet

the battle
it rages on

still

I am sad

and waiting

epilogue

(not) by accident

today

I had a revelation

today

the outline of my soul

revealed itself

in the bloody incestines

of my victim

I saw it there

and it stared right back

at me

surprising me

I didn't expect

that

I didn't expect

me

not yet

not now

Credits

Writer: j. t. baka.

Written (analogue): from the 15th of September 2018 to the 1st of March 2020.

Written (digital): from the 16th of September 2018 to the 31st of March 2020.

Pictures: Simon Wagenschütz.

Editorial deadline (lyrics): the 20th of April 2020.

in memoriam

becoming darth vader

sitting

in a train

near the washroom

watching

people open the door

fully

that stands open 70% already

watching

people trying to close the door

fully

after stepping inside the washroom

but the door

stopps at 70%

every time

the people

are trying

one time two times three times

to close

the door

until

they resort to the use of force

and the door

relents

welcome to the dark side

Impressum

Redaktionsschluss: 03.05.2020.

©2020 baka, j. t.
Herstellung und Verlag: BoD - Books on Demand,
Norderstedt.

ISBN-13: 9783751919975.